About the author

Jill Reece was a qualified primary school teacher in Kent for many years before changing to Social Services, where she became responsible for providing care to older people in their own homes. This is her third publication based totally on work life experiences. She lives in Suffolk with her husband, three cats and four chickens. She has one daughter and two grown up grandchildren.

To Irene
Best wishes
from
Jill Reece

Condensed Milk And Pickled Onions

Jill Reece

Condensed Milk And Pickled Onions

Vanguard Press

A CIP catalogue record for this title is
available from the British Library.

ISBN 978 1 784653 84 2

*Vanguard Press is an imprint of
Pegasus Elliot MacKenzie Publishers Ltd.*
www.pegasuspublishers.com

First Published in 2018

**Vanguard Press
Sheraton House Castle Park
Cambridge England**

Printed & Bound in Great Britain

Dedication

To my husband, Barry, who has always been there for me over the years.

Love you.

Condensed Milk and Pickled Onions

My heart was literally pounding as I ducked under the car park barrier. I mean it's not every day that you are asked to go and persuade a notorious elderly "bag lady" that she needs your help. Mrs Austin was living in a once blue Cortina. The car sat sheltered under the huge concrete sea wall parked all alone in an abandoned car park. I say sheltered, but dark green stains ran down the wall, evidence of sea water that had tumbled over the top on many occasions. As I walked towards the car my feet crunched on piles of sea strewn pebbles and lumps of dried seaweed. The dried black bladder wrack made popping noises as my feet trod on the air-filled pouches. As I approached the Cortina, I could just make out a shape inside it, so I tapped on the passenger door window and a face turned to look at me. The face belonged to a female of undecipherable age. I was worried about her safety as the old car was the only vehicle in the park, and it stuck out like a sore thumb.

'Go away,' she said and turned away from me. The wind off the incoming tide tumbled over the wall and blew my hair all over my face. It was fairly obvious that she wasn't going to invite me in, but I am one of those people who never gives up. I tapped on the window again.

'Mrs Austin, I have come to talk to you. I want to tell you about a ground floor flat in that block just over there,' I said, pointing roughly in the direction of the flats. 'One of the very nice ground floor flats has just become vacant and the Council and I both think that we should offer you the first chance to take it. You would certainly be warmer and safer there than here in this car. It would be nice and warm and you would have lots of room to store all your stuff.' I had already noted the huge black bags stuffed to bursting on the back seats. 'Would you like to consider that?'

I hoped she would, as with much worse winter weather forecast I didn't like the idea of an elderly lady living in this clapped-out car. I walked round to the driver's side and tried the handle. It gave a bit and the door opened. I asked if I might get in out of the cold wind.

'I don't care what you do,' she snapped. So I got in the driver's seat, and there we sat in the dirty cold car under the sea wall glaring at each other. I must admit the inside was a lot warmer than the outside.

'You would be a lot more comfortable in the flat than here in the car,' I said'

'What do you know about how comfortable I am?'

I shrugged and showed her some pictures of the flat and its contents. It was really one very large room, with a kitchenette in one end, which had a sink unit and a gas cooker. Space for the bed was at the other end. The heating was provided as part of the rent, so there would be no trouble about keeping her warm. The previous tenant had left all the curtains at the two large windows, and the floor was carpeted in a fawn very clean carpet. All she would need was an armchair or small settee, a bed, and any other small bits and pieces that she wanted once she was in residence.

'I'll think about it,' she said, 'Come and see me next week and I will give you my answer.'

I felt just like a servant being addressed by the lady of the manor.

Luckily for her, she accepted the offer and within two weeks was moved in with her meagre belongings. I made very quick arrangements for the car to be towed away before she changed her mind. My home helps got together and furnished the flat with an assortment of odds and ends, from a small fund that they had created some months earlier. They had all agreed to put five pounds each into a kitty so that any elderly person that they visited who was in need could purchase some essentials from the fund. They were extremely careful how the money was spent, and often trawled round the local shops for free items or negotiated with shopkeepers for really good second-hand prices. Mrs Austin received a used fridge and a new microwave from the local electrical shop. We found her some bedding and a nice clean mattress. She settled in quickly and we all thought we would have a peaceful time with her. What a mistake, for here began a long and fraught time dealing with her eccentric behaviour.

I picked one of my best most experienced home helps to assist her. I explained how eccentric she might be and we discussed what sort of behaviour might arise. I knew from the helper's previous clients that she would cope with almost anything.

The bad behaviour took all sorts of routes. Firstly she would put the gas on and not light it for ages. She would open her front door so that the smell would permeate through the hall and upstairs to the other flats. The other residents, of course, phoned the police. Then she would often lock the front access door from the inside and leave her key in it so nobody else could get access to the building. Then she acquired a radio which she put on at two or three in the morning as loud as it would go. The complaints came in thick and fast. Both myself and the police were inundated with reports of her behaviour. A couple of years later she had a nasty bout of bronchitis and was confined to bed for a week. She sent the home help out to buy three tins of condensed milk and two jars of pickled onions.

'I only want "Carnation" milk', she insisted, 'It's the thickest and best'.

'Open the tins and leave them on my bedside table,' she demanded.

After the home help had left for the day she got out of bed, drizzled the condensed milk all-round the skirting

12

board of her main room. Then she drained the pickled onions, sat in her armchair and threw the pickled onions at the lines of milk. If the onions stuck in the milk she gave herself ten points. If they rolled off but had touched the sticky milk she gave herself five points, if she missed which she didn't very often she got no points. She had a little notebook and pencil for keeping track of her scores.

I leave you to imagine the scene after the weekend when the home help arrived. Mrs Austin was full of delight with her various scores, and wanted the home help to join in the game. The smell of the onions and vinegar almost overwhelmed her. It was impossible to clean up the condensed milk. Months later it had walked itself across the room and our shoes picked up the sticky goo. She absolutely refused to have a new carpet, or to stop playing the game. The home help had a pair of shoes which she wore only for Mrs Austin's property and then changed outside her door into another pair. The onion game lasted a long time. The home help had to pick them out of the goo, wash them and return them to the jar for the next round. The carpet just got stickier and stickier. You would not believe the noise it made as you walked across the room.

She had put a set of jumbo rollers in her hair which were there for so long that her hair grew through them and she sported a huge head of hair that didn't match her frail small face. It made her look even more peculiar than usual.

Her health gradually deteriorated, and one day the helper phoned to say she couldn't get in to the flat the door was locked from the inside.

We left it for a day, thinking that she was having one of her "off" days, but when it wasn't unlocked the next day I called round to the police station and a huge young policeman accompanied me to the flat. We couldn't open the front door so we went out in the garden and noticed that the kitchen window was unlatched. What happened next was just like a farce. The policeman cupped his hands together and suggested that he lift me up to the kitchen window. I could then open the front door and let him in. Although the flat was on the ground floor the land dipped at the back which made the window about six feet up. Too high to look in but low enough for me to be lifted into. I wasn't exactly dressed for a spot of mountain climbing, and worried about the view of my behind as I scrambled up, but I duly stepped into the policeman's cupped hands and clambered in through the window and over the draining board of the sink. I opened the door and let him in. There was a very still shape in the bed.

'Mrs Austin,' I called. No response. The policeman gently pulled back the covers and peeped at her.

'She's gone I think,' he said. We proceeded to look round the flat for any documents that would help us to begin the organizing of the necessary processes. We were both whispering to each other as we went about our business. I'm not exactly sure why we whisper in the presence of the dead but we all do. After about twenty minutes, as we were standing with our backs to the bed,

Mrs. Austin suddenly rose silently up behind us and yelled 'FUCK OFF'

And that's exactly what we did. He went out of the door like a bat out of hell, but I for some unknown reason exited the way I had come in, via the sink unit. I fell out of the window into the long course grass of the garden. Why I didn't follow the policeman out the door I will never know. He came running round and picked me up out of the grass. I can't imagine what he wrote about me in his report.

The home help, the policeman, and I were the only people at her funeral when she died a few weeks later. It was exactly the same kind of weather on the day of her funeral as it was on the first day I met her in the old Cortina. But we all missed her eccentricities, and life in general calmed down considerably

Her helper missed her more than she was prepared to say and would often call into the office about someone, but always referred to Mrs Austin with great affection. She had thrown away her sticky shoes though.

Charlie Chaplin's Sister

I was asked to visit an elderly lady who, I was informed, was believed to be Charlie Chaplin's sister. She lived way out on the cliffs in a very remote part of the island facing the North Sea. All it said on the referral was that she had a load of cats. Now I am an avid cat lover so I was quite looking forward to seeing what a load of cats meant.

It took me ages to find the bungalow because it was so remote and when I did find it I was totally shocked. Here was a once lovely double fronted bay windowed property with absolutely no glass in any of the windows. The cruel wind off the sea was blowing directly into the open casements. Tatty curtains were flapping in the gaps were the glass used to be. The front door was wide open so I stepped inside calling out for Miss Baker. My feet crunched in about four inches of a dry dusty substance, which covered every surface. Then I found out what a load of cats actually meant. There were cats everywhere: on the floor, on the windowsills, on the couch, on the chairs, they all looked at me wide-eyed. There must have been fifty or so of them. In the middle of the couch covered in felines sat a little old lady. She was so small I almost missed her. I noticed immediately that she was dressed in an overcoat, hat and scarf.

'Hallo my dear,' she said, 'What can I do for you?'

'Well actually I've come to see if I can do something for you,' I replied.

'Please sit down, dear'.

I sat and was immediately covered in cats. They sat on my lap, on my shoulders, on my briefcase. They sat everywhere. Then I noticed one tiny little dog in amongst them.

'That's Pluto, he's totally blind,' she told me.

I couldn't help thinking that might just be an advantage in his situation. By this time it had dawned on me that the crunchy stuff all over the floors was dried cats' poo, and yet there was no cat smell anywhere. I suppose with that much fresh air constantly blowing in there wouldn't be a smell.

'Are you really Charlie Chaplin's sister?' I asked, I couldn't help myself.

'Oh yes, but I never really had much to do with him. We were a really odd family as families go. To be quite honest we didn't have much to do with each other even when we were small children.

'I would like you to come outside and see my garden' she said, 'It is so peaceful I just love being out there. I love to hear the birds singing but they never seem to come into the garden, for some reason. I do wish they would.'

'I'm not surprised,' I replied. 'There are cats' eyes gleaming behind every clump of grass. Only a really daft bird would consider landing in here.'

'I suppose you're right,' she replied. We went back into the house.

As the north wind whistled through the house we talked about what I might be able to do for her. My first thought was to get glass put into all the windows.

'I like my windows to be left open for the cats to come and go as they please. With so many of them it saves me having to keep getting up to let them in or out.'

'You could have a cat flap or even two.'

'Oh no, dear, they wouldn't like that, all that squeezing through small gaps.'

Dr. Perkins had put on his referral that she wouldn't need any meals on wheels as she had just cooked a roast for herself on the day he called.

I asked if I might look in the kitchen. It was like going into one of the guano caves on the Galapagos Islands. The cooker had huge cobwebs all over it and the electric plates were eaten away with rust. Huge spiders scuttled away from me into their dense hanging webs. I knew without a shadow of doubt that his lady hadn't cooked a roast on that cooker for some time. I was really angry with the doctor for not noticing what a state the cooker was in. How could he not have noticed the rust and the cobwebs?

I decided that food was the best thing I could arrange first so I ordered Meals on Wheels. I imagined if she got used to those I could introduce a clean-up at a later date.

My first priority was the windows. I managed to get the Department of Health and Social Security to pay for the glass but I couldn't find anyone who would put it in for free. So my long suffering husband offered to do it for me.

The glass duly arrived and off he went. All of her window frames were rotten from being left open in all weathers. So he put the glass in and nailed the window frames shut, to stop the glass from falling straight out. While he was there Miss Baker put her hat and coat on and looked as though she was going somewhere.

'Are you off?' asked my husband.

'Oh, yes, I am walking up to Warden Point to get my pension and some cat food.'

'Isn't that rather a long way?' he asked as he nailed a window into place.

'It's only three miles there and three back.'

Well he couldn't just let her walk three miles out and three miles back could he? So he offered to give her a lift, and off they went. Whilst parked outside the post office, a beady-eyed-policeman came along on a bike and asked my husband what he was doing sitting in a scruffy van outside the post office. Obviously he thought he was going to rob it or something. My husband's old van was a very unlikely getaway car.

After explaining why he was sitting outside the policeman noticed that one of the tyres was rather balder than it should have been; having pointed this out to my husband he told him to get it replaced.

Miss Baker came out of the post office with two heavy trays of cat food. How she would have got them three miles home nobody knows. She might have purchased more because she knew she had a lift, of course.

When my husband went back a few days later to see how the glass had fared, and to finish the task, he was horrified. Even though he had instructed her not to open the windows, Miss Baker had opened all the frames and the glass was nowhere to be seen unless you looked out of the windows and down to the piles of shattered bits on the ground.

He came home in despair. And two weeks later received a forty-pound fine in the post for having a bald tyre on his van. So much for being so helpful.

I have to say he was less than pleased.

From Cold to Hot

It was a freezing cold day when I was asked to visit Miss Carter. Snow flurries were hurtling towards my car windscreen and my wipers had some trouble whisking it from left to right. I was as warm as toast with my car heater working on double strength.

Why is it that each time the weather was inclement I was always having to drive up one of the many unmade roads on the island. This one was particularly bad, being really nothing more than a series of huge potholes, and scattered with loose stones.

I found the bungalow, just as I expected it would be, totally isolated and set back from the cart track in an overgrown garden.

A note in spidery writing said "Please call to back door". The number of times I have told elderly residents not to do that, but they never seemed to understand the dangers.

I buttoned up my coat, pulled on my hat and gloves and made my way to the back door.

Inside was like an ice box. Seated in a huge armchair was the tiniest little old lady I had ever seen. She wore a coat, hat, and mittens. A big hand-knitted scarf was wound round her neck and she peered out at me as I came into the room. The fire grate had newspaper and a small amount of kindling in it but it was not lit.

'Why haven't you lit your fire?' I asked.

'It doesn't matter, my dear I'm not really cold; I have my lovely coat and scarf on so I won't be needing the fire.'

'But if you lit the fire you would be much cosier.'

'Well the trouble is, my dear, I haven't been able to get out to get my pension and I haven't got any matches.'

I don't smoke so I had no matches or lighter with me or in the car. The decision was just being made in my head that I would go down the lane to the nearest shop and get her pension and some matches when there was a noise at the back door. In bounced a man dressed in a long black gown and cloak. He also sported a huge black woolly hat, a scarf and woollen gloves. His breath formed little clouds of vapour as he puffed from the exertion of coming up her drive.

'Oh, hello Vicar' said Miss Carter. How are you today? I see it is snowing. Now why have you taken the time and trouble to come all the way from the vicarage to see me today?'

I was expecting him to say that he had come to offer any help she was requiring. He managed not to even ask who I was. It was just as though I was invisible.

'Well, Miss Carter, you have been a bit remiss; you haven't paid for your parish magazine for a few weeks now. So I've called to collect your payment. I know you won't want to get behind will you?'

'Oh, my goodness, Vicar, I'm so sorry. How much do I owe you?'

'Two pounds. I'm afraid.'

'Get my purse for me dear, would you?' she asked me, 'It's on the sideboard in the kitchen.' I went into her kitchen and returned with the purse; she paid him, and much to my amazement he took the two pounds and left.

I was furious. How could he have come in all wrapped up against the cold and just walked away leaving her in this frozen house?

'Right,' I said, 'I'm going to go down to the post office and I will get your pension, and some matches. Is there anything else you need?'

'I could do with some food,' she said in a very small voice.

'Write me out a list and sign the pension book to allow me to collect it for you and I will be back.'

Whilst she wrote out her shopping list in her spidery hand I looked round the room. All the furnishings were heavy, mostly antique, and well looked after. A very threadbare carpet covered most of the floor, and I noticed several ragged places where she could easily trip, but I expect she knew the places very well and avoided them.

When I got to the post office in the nearest village the lady behind the counter told me that Miss Carter hadn't collected her pension for some long time, eight weeks in fact.

'We were a bit worried about her,' the post office lady said. I returned loaded with money, a few bits of shopping and six boxes of matches. As soon as I got back I lit the fire and it soon blazed up giving off its rays of warmth.

As we filled out the forms for her to have some help each week I realized that I was beginning to shout. I was beginning to shout because there was a roaring sound coming from up the chimney. I expect you know what I am going to say next. In my eagerness to warm up the room, I had let the fire blaze too quickly and had set the chimney alight. I went outside to look back at the chimney pot. There were flames coming out of the pot, along with plumes of thick black smoke. I went back indoors and shovelled a whole pile of ashes onto the fire, luckily for me, it cooled the blaze down and the flames stopped. I didn't need to call the fire brigade. I waited for it to cool down further, then relit the fire with a much smaller quantity of wood and coal. I refilled her coal scuttle from a pile of frozen coal outside the back door, and left when I knew the fire was safe and warming her nicely.

I arranged for her chimney to be swept, and a home help to call every day to light the fire and make sure she had both her pension and her food shopping. She loved having the helper mostly for the company that the service gave her. Next time I visited the fire was alight and Miss Carter was a very happy lady.

But I was still cross with the vicar.

Hell on Earth

The referral from Doctor York read, "Please visit this very overweight lady who has heart problems and finds caring for her husband rather difficult."

This one would be a doddle that could be left till after lunch, I thought.

The bungalow was a semi-detached fairly modern council property, within a stone's throw of the gates to the General Hospital. The ubiquitous note on the front door said "Please call at back door".

I walked into the kitchen which was quite small, and I was overwhelmed with the presence of the largest lady I have ever encountered in my life. She was huge. She completely filled the kitchen. I explained why I had come and she immediately went into a raft of things she didn't like about her husband. He wouldn't according to her do anything for himself and left her to do everything. As she calmed down having got all the moans off her chest she invited me to follow her to the lounge.

It was a very pleasant property, but there was a pervading smell that I just couldn't place. It was sweet and yet it was sour. It wasn't urine or anything worse, it reminded me of strawberries and lemon juice. I noticed it as soon as I went in the kitchen door but through into the lounge it was almost suffocating.

Seated in an old upright wheelchair was a man I presumed was Mr. Darby. He was dressed in a brown tweed suit and had one of those highly coloured crocheted blankets over his legs. His face was gaunt and grey coloured.

As we began to talk about her needs for help I realized that Mr. Darby was contributing nothing to the conversation, even when his wife was complaining loudly about his inability to do anything.

'He has sat in that bloody wheelchair for the last few months. He doesn't even get up to go to the toilet he just wets himself and I have to clean up after him.' Mr Darby still took no part in the discussion. I worked out a help programme that I thought would suit them. I knelt down in front of the wheelchair to try to engage him in conversation, assuming that perhaps he might be totally deaf. As our eyes met I saw abject terror in his eyes. I had never seen such a reaction before. He totally confused me. Whatever could be scaring him so much? I assumed that at least if a helper got in there tomorrow I could find out from her what the situation was in the house. I wondered if his huge wife was hurting him or worse. Was he just terrified of authority?

I was still in a confused state when I left the bungalow. As I went out to my car I saw a district nurse whom I knew well coming out of the bungalow next door.

'Have you got a minute to look at this couple?' I asked. She came from the same surgery as the referring GP so I thought it would be OK for her to look.

"Sure,' she said 'What's the problem?'

'I don't really know but something just isn't right and there's a smell I can't place.'

We walked up to the kitchen door together laughing about her son's love life, but as soon as she opened the kitchen door she went green and said 'Oh my God!'

'What?' I asked. 'Do you think you know what that smell is?'

'I don't think I know, I know I know.' She said, 'It's gangrene.'

I had read several times about the unique smell of gangrene but never having experienced it before I didn't recognise it.

We both went back into the lounge. Nurse knelt down in front of Mr Darby and gently put her hand on his knees. The sharp intake of breath that escaped from him will live with me forever. It was total agony, let out in one long breath. Nurse removed the coloured blanket which was soaked with liquid. She took out a pair of scissors from her case and gently cut up the legs of Mr Darby's trousers. What she exposed made me gag and I had to run out into the garden and throw up my sandwich lunch. His leg bones were exposed all the way from his knees to his feet. The flesh around the bones was black, blue, yellow green and all the colours of the rainbow. This poor man must have been in agony for months. His legs were literally rotten.

Nurse went straight out to their hall and phoned for an ambulance. I heard her saying that ten minutes would not do, she wanted it now.

The ambulance came from just round the corner. The paramedics wanted to move him out of his wheelchair into one of their special carrying chairs, but Nurse insisted that he was not to be moved from it. Off he went.

'He won't be coming back,' she said as we walked out to our cars. 'He won't survive the amputations.'

She was right he didn't.

The situation ate into my brain for days I was so cross that Dr. York hadn't even recognized the gangrene smell. Surely he should have known something wasn't right.

He was famous for rolling up his trouser legs and standing in the sea early every morning before surgery hours. He professed that it made him sturdy and healthy. So I got up early and drove down to the sea the following morning and although it was October I rolled up my trouser legs and waded in till I was right next to him.

'I've come to discuss the situation at Mr. and Mrs. Darby's house,' I said. 'How could you have left that house without so much as acknowledging that there was a major problem with Mr Darby, not just a domestic problem for his wife?'

'How dare you speak to me about my diagnosis. Who do you think you are? I shall be visiting Mr Darby today as it happens although it isn't any of your business.'

'I wouldn't bother if I was you, doctor; Mr. Darby died last night, having both legs amputated.'

I flounced out of the freezing cold sea, satisfied that I had scored a point on Mr. Darby's behalf.

It took about half an hour for the feeling to come back into my legs and feet, but I felt the agony was worth it.

The Milk Children

I visited a charming elderly lady who lived in a three storey house on the seafront. She was a pure genteel middle class Victorian, so polite and worried about me sitting in one of her old armchairs, that she hadn't dusted since yesterday.

She was really lovely and spoke about her many years in Kenya where she worked as a nurse in one of the missionary hospitals. Her room was filled with artefacts from Africa and other exotic places. As we discussed what her immediate needs were she explained that she got very depressed because she couldn't keep the huge house up to the standard she expected of herself.

'I'm not that surprised, looking at your birth date you are eighty-six Miss Edwards.' I said hoping to make her feel better.

'Well it's not me I'm worried about, my dear; it's all my children in the front room.'

'Your children?'

'Yes you see I have so many to care for and I'm worried what will happen to them if I can't look after them.'

I wasn't quite sure what we were talking about at this point so I asked if I could see the children.

'Oh yes, of course, you can. Maybe you would like to care for some of them if you have the time.'

I followed her out of the back room towards the front bay windowed room. She opened the door and we went in. The whole room was full of bottles of milk. There must have been a couple of hundred. Some of them had gone mouldy and the milk had risen up three or four inches, with the silver foil tops sticking up in the air.

'Aren't they just beautiful?' she asked.

I was speechless for a few moments. I mean, what could I say?

'How long have they been here?' was all I could think of.

'It varies; some of them have been here since I retired from Kenya, whilst others have come to me for care quite recently.'

I looked at the rows and rows of bottles. They were on every surface all over the floor, all along the large window sills. Some of the milk was clearly rotten but amazingly there was no rancid smell.

I put some help in to keep the rest of the house clean but the helper was instructed not to go into the front room (which of course she did when I wasn't there, and Miss Edwards was not looking).

Miss Edwards passed peacefully away some months later and it fell to me to get the local dairy to come and collect the bottles. There were five hundred and eighty-four of them. Some were as old as 1952. Some of them found a place in the local museum. The rest were crushed at the glass works and turned into car windscreens. So, some of Miss Edwards' children are still being very useful even today.

Lots of Very Cold Water

Mr. Fuller was a famous Irish resident of the island. He got very belligerent when he had too much to drink, which was almost a daily occurrence.

He had a wonderful helper who coped with his erratic and often offensive behaviour (because she knew even more swear words than he did). They seemed to be able to understand each other's limits.

One very cold winter's night the tide, driven by ferocious winds, overflowed the sea defenses and the road Mr. Fuller lived in was awash with waist high water.

We set up a feeding station on dry land with the WRVS, cooking a hot meal for anyone without power. I was asked by the police if there was anyone I was worried about, and I immediately thought of Mr Fuller and his two dogs. They would all be hungry. So I gathered three steak pie and chips meals, covered them with thick wrapping paper and the fire brigade took me in a rubber dinghy down the flooded road to Mr. Fuller's house. One of the firemen lifted me out of the boat and put me on the front windowsill. He turned out not to be one of life's most tactful of men for he said, 'Blimey I didn't think you'd be that heavy.'

That was the moment that I decided to go on yet another diet. I stood on the windowsill pulled the sash window up and stepped into the front room. To this day I cannot tell you why, but I didn't expect the water in the house to be as deep as the water outside. I went up to my waist in freezing cold water. They passed me the meals and I waded across the room remembering all the hazardous electric cables that usually ran all over the floor. On the stairs, at the edge of the water, stood the dogs, wagging their tails and whimpering. I dished out two of the steak pie and chips meals onto the first dry stair, about half way up the flight, and left them chomping in great delight whilst I climbed up to Mr. Fuller's bedroom. He was in bed, blurry eyes with an empty bottle of Scotch beside him.

'What the fuck do you want?' he said in his best slurred voice.

'I thought you might be hungry so I've brought you steak pie and chips'

'How the hell did you get in here?'

'I came up the road in a boat and got in through your front window.'

'Well you can piss off and shut the bloody window on your way out.'

I left him knowing that he wouldn't come to much harm without eating his steak pie and chips hot. He could eat it later when he found it by his bed.

Several months before the floods his wife had died and I sorted out the available "Death Grant" of forty pounds for him to help towards burial costs. Three weeks after the supposed funeral date I called in to see how he was coping on his own, and there in the front bedroom was the wife, unburied. He had drunk the forty pounds and done nothing about her burial. I couldn't get another grant out of the DHSS so it came out of the home helps' charity fund. His home help and I made sure she got buried this time as we had a police escort. Mr. Fuller didn't come; he was too drunk to get dressed, and we wouldn't let him accompany us in his tatty pyjamas.

Later, of course, we had all the cleaning up after the flood. We found him some furniture that was in a skip down the road. He thought it was very good quality, and so it was.

He behaved himself for some time after all the excitement of the flooding. I know that his home help went miles past her brief to ensure that he ate a hot meal and didn't have too many bottles of whiskey in the kitchen.

My Auntie Margaret

One of my special tasks was debt collecting. If anyone had not paid for some time for their service it was down to me to go and try to collect the outstanding monies. I really hated this part of my job.

On this day I had to go to a very remote part of the island where years ago people had built bungalows and houses for holidays and retirement without any planning permission. It wasn't required in those days. Now with partners dead and gone, many, mostly elderly women, found themselves alone in these remote isolated properties. One such lady was a Mrs, Grant. She wasn't a client of mine but had the service some time ago when her husband was ill in bed. She owed in excess of £200.

As I pulled up outside the house I felt that it was looking at me with its bleak black windows. They looked just like angry eyes. My heart sank. I got out of the car and approached the front door. The knocker seemed to echo through the house. I waited whilst a selection of bolts were being undone from the inside the door opened to reveal an elderly lady. She was very tall and straight. She was wearing one of those wrap around aprons, in a floral pink and yellow pattern. She had fine grey hair pinned back in a bun.

'What do you want?'

'If I may come in, Mrs. Grant, perhaps we could discuss a sum of money that you owe to the Council.

She let me in and much to my consternation she bolted all the bolts behind me turned the key in the lock and dropped the key into her apron pocket.

As I am somewhat claustrophobic I wasn't too keen on this.

We had a long discussion about her debt which she promised to pay if the council sorted out the problem she had brought to their attention.

'What problem is that?' I enquired. I wish I hadn't asked.

'Well I have noticed that the council are making heavy water and spreading it along the verges in the lane. I see them early in the morning before anyone else is up. They needn't think I haven't seen.'

'Heavy water?'

'Yes, just look at the verges do you see how all the bushes are going brown?'

'It is autumn Mrs. Grant. The trees and bushes are losing their leaves because it's autumn.'

'Rubbish! I know what they're up to.'

We sat in silence for a while and she said menacingly, 'Of course, now that I've been silly enough to let you into the big secret I don't see how I can just let you go.'

My heart did a cartwheel and my mind began to whirl.

'If only I could let Central Government know I'm sure Mrs. Thatcher would do something about this and put a stop to it.'

It was then that my mind burst into action. Devious it might have been but it was to get me out of the house.

'Ah I might be able to help you there. You see Mrs. Thatcher is my Auntie Margaret and I am having tea with her on Sunday afternoon. If you were to write all this down in a letter and seal it I will deliver it to her for you and then she will know.'

I sat in silence for the next hour while she wrote out her big secret in a fine cultured hand, using pen and ink. She sealed the envelope and placed it into my waiting hands; I hoped that now the locks and bolts would all be undone to let me out, and they were.

I have never driven away from a house as fast as I did from that one. I think I could have qualified for a good place in a Formula One racing grid.

A Longing in my Loins

The district nurse and I decided to this visit together as we both needed to see what was required of our joint services. The house was in a dreadful state. The paint had peeled off the front door and the window many years ago. Curtains that hung at the window looked like dirty old sacking. It was a terraced house and either side were beautifully kept with shiny paint and cleaned windows, there was even a hanging basket to the right with colourful petunias.

'Why do we always have to go into the revolting houses,' the Nurse said as we knocked at the door.

A scruffy dishevelled man answered the door. He had a crop of wiry red hair, bloodshot eyes and a huge ginger moustache.

'Ah, ladies, come in. It's not often I have the services of two ladies at a time.'

We should have known then what was in store, but in we went.

'Have a seat,' he said pointing to one old leather armchair. The nurse sat in the chair and I perched on the arm. It was then that I noticed five chamber pots all filled to various levels with urine placed along the hearth in front of the fireplace.

'Why are you keeping urine in those pots?' I asked.

'Because, Doctor told me to keep an eye on my urine for a week, and to see if there was any change in the colour from day to day. So that's this week's Monday to Friday. They all look the same to me but Doctor will obviously be able to see what's what.'

We both stared at the urine. After we had explained what services were on offer, he decided that didn't want a home help interfering in his life, and he had nothing of any health nature for the nurse to do. It was then that I stupidly asked the obvious question but immediately wished that I hadn't.

'Is there anything either of us can do for you whilst we are both here?'

As the words left my mouth I knew we were in for trouble. He stood up, pulled down his trousers and revealed one of the biggest male appendages I had ever seen.

'I've got this awful longing in my loins, ladies I don't know if either of you would like to help me out?

The nurse got up from the chair so fast it immediately toppled me off the arm and we beat a hasty retreat to the front door. I trod on the back of her heels twice in our flight. There was an alley beside the row of houses, and we both belted round into it almost collapsing with laughter. A woman who walked past us must have been puzzled at the sight of a district nurse in full uniform, and a woman in a business suit laughing as if fit to burst.

Needless to say I was glad that I didn't have to let one of my lovely ladies into that situation.

A Wandering Wife

I visited an elderly couple having been asked by their doctor to provide some help for the ninety-one-year-old husband caring for his severely demented wife.

Within a few minutes of meeting him he had me in tears. Here he was at his age loading the washing machine with their bed linen as his wife soiled the sheets every night. He didn't once complain about his lot, but as he described her descent into dementia a huge tear rolled down his cheek (and so one or two rolled down mine too).

'I'm totally ashamed of myself,' he said wiping the tears from his eyes. 'I ought to be able to care for my wife now, after all she has cared for me throughout the years.'

'I'm sure you are caring for her Mr Ibden.' as I spoke his wife entered the room. She was immaculately attired in a very smart beige dress with a string of pearls at her neck. Her hair was shining and combed, she reminded me of a fine example of a dowager duchess.

'She's nearly ninety,' her husband offered.

They sat together on the upright settee, holding hands, and presenting a picture of Victoriana in its heyday.

'The trouble is she wanders. If I turn my back for one moment she's out of the front door and away. Aren't you, my Love?' She just smiled at him with a very disarming smile. 'The police have had to bring her back several times. It's such a worry. I daren't even go to the toilet without making sure she is here.'

'Obviously you have tried locking the front door,' I said, knowing that the answer would be yes.

'She knows how to unlock it, and even if I hide the keys she seems to be able to find them. It's very difficult for me.'

'Look, if I arrange for a lady to come in and help you by taking over the washing and the ironing, shopping and any of the other tedious tasks do you think that will help with the strain?'

'Do you think I deserve that kind of help?'

'Deserve? Of course you deserve,' I replied. What else could I say?

I chose a lovely helper for them and he was so grateful he kept trying to pay her by putting money in her bag when she wasn't looking. In the end she had to go through her belongings before she left the house in case he had stuffed cash into her pockets.

Mrs. Ibden kept up her wanderings and once was taken off a train going to the mainland. She was only taken off because she didn't have a ticket. Then it got even worse because she began to wander in the middle of the night. She was found wandering in her nightdress with bare feet almost two miles away from the house. Then she got out of her bath while Mr Ibden was fetching a warmed towel and went out in the street totally naked.

Everyone began to talk about her going into a care home, but Mr Ibden was having none of it. He insisted that he could cope. I increased his level of help to make sure that he could.

Down at the police station they had a picture of her on the wall, with her name and address, so that all the police officers and staff could recognise her if they saw her out alone.

Then some time later Mr. Ibden phoned and sounded very mysterious.

'I've solved the wandering problem,' he said laughingly.

'Wow! Tell me more.'

'No, I'm not giving away the secret on the phone. Come and look,'

I went straight round to the house. He led me back towards the front door. There emblazoned on the back of the door was a sign, beautifully designed with proper lettering. It said "Gentlemen's Toilet".

'Well she won't go through there now. She wouldn't dare go into a men's toilet. So she hasn't wandered now for five weeks. I can't tell you what a relief it is to me.'

So the answer unable to be found by all of us so called professionals was simple and found by the carer himself, mainly because he knew very well that his wife would not enter a gentleman's toilet.

A Brush or Two with Post-Natal Depression

Not every client that I was asked to help was elderly. I was often asked to help new mums cope with the arrival of their first baby. Sometimes these mums would have been diagnosed with post-natal depression. This varied enormously in its symptoms. I was asked to visit a new mum in the warder's housing complex at the local open prison. I had to leave my car in the visitor's park as I was not authorised to drive into the housing complex.

I found the flat and knocked at the door. The lady who opened the door was about thirty. She looked like she was under some stress, but then most new mums do. I sat and talked to her for a while and asked if I could see the baby. I noticed that she didn't pick it up to show me; she told me to look in the pram.

'Is it a boy or a girl?' I asked as it was too small for me to decide.

'A girl,' she replied. 'My husband wanted a boy, and he's a bit disappointed.'

As I got into the paper filling part of the visit I asked her for verification of her income.

'I will go upstairs and get the information,' she said, and off she went.

I stayed looking at the baby fascinated by how small it was. I had totally forgotten just how small newborn babies were. After some time I realized that she must be having trouble finding the documents so I called up the stairs to see if she needed any help. There was no answer. I went up to the top floor but there was nobody there at all. I was alone with the baby. I nearly died of fright. What best to do? I walked across to the prison building, taking the baby asleep in the pram with me and asked to speak to someone in authority. It was some years since I had pushed a pram! An assistant warden told me that Mr. Jones, the husband, was away on a course and they couldn't or wouldn't be able to help. What a caring workplace I thought. There was nothing for it but to go back to the flat and phone the social services duty officer, using the flat's phone. Luckily for me the duty officer was a friend of mine and she set up an urgent call to come and fetch the baby.

I had to sit in the flat with the baby until an emergency foster parent turned up to collect it. We searched the flat for clothes, bottles, etc and finally off went the lady with the baby and all its belongings.

I wrote to the prison governor immediately stating how distressed I was at the lack of help and understanding of his staff. His answer, when it eventually arrived, was as lacking in sympathy as his staff's original responses.

Apparently when the husband returned from his course, not having been informed of the events, he collected his baby daughter from the foster lady, resigned from his job and went to live with his parents. So I suppose that was a happy ending, at least it was for the baby. The mother was found wandering in Scotland, how she got there we do not know. She had some hospital care but did not return to her husband. He cared for the baby as a single dad and did a good job.

The second baby problem was in the army barracks. A newly delivered mum had severe depression and couldn't even pick her baby up. The husband was quite high up in the rankings and could not understand where his wife was coming from. I insisted that he was present when I visited, and I'm glad he was because he was the major part of the problem.

'Surely she can cope with a baby,' he said, 'After all she wanted a baby. I most certainly did not. Now it's here she can't cope. You women really are peculiar creatures.'

I tried to explain about post-natal depression but he didn't want to hear.

'Well don't expect me to do anything about this I've got troops to train and I can't spare any time with this nonsense,' and with that he stormed out.

I went to see the camp commander and explained what was happening. He was very sympathetic and suggested that he could move the arrogant husband to a course away from home for three months while we put help in for the wife. This worked a treat and soon she was as happy with her baby as she could be. The helper made a whole lot of difference, but I honestly think it was the absence of the husband that helped most.

One Bad Apple

It is inevitable that in a huge team of employees every now and then one bad apple will turn up. And so it was with my team. Home helps are put in the path of many temptations especially when handling money. Some elderly people appear to them to have cartloads of money that they don't or won't spend.

Usually if placed in a sticky situation they would either pop into the office to report the issue or phone in. Either way I would visit while the helper was at the house to discuss the situation with both helper an client. Normally we sorted something out which meant the cash wasn't lying around for all and sundry to see.

One fairly new helper was causing me some concerns. I have to say that prior to an interview I always drove past the address of an applicant just to see what kind of housing they lived in and mostly to look at the upkeep of their own house. This often told me a lot about the person applying to help others. This particular lady lived in a rather dilapidated house with an overgrown garden, but of course, not having met her she might well have been a single parent or divorcee trying to cope alone. She came in for the interview and got the job on merit. She seemed to have all the right attitudes and answers to the care questions. She worked well and hard for quite a while. Her clients spoke very highly of her. It was after some months whilst visiting one of her clients that as we spoke about her the client praised her to the skies but sowed a seed of doubt in my mind, because just as I was leaving the client said, 'She's really good to me; she keeps my savings books at her house because she's got a safe and she says they are safer locked away.'

The home help then popped into the office to ask if she could have a fortnight off as she had "Won a Holiday to the Bahamas". The girls in the office were really happy for her but I had misgivings stirring in the back of my mind. I kept thinking about those bank books. I gave her the fortnight off on the condition that she gave me Mrs. King's bank books. She went a bit pale, but she came in with them the next day. When I looked through them there was a debit for four thousand pounds from her Scottish savings bond account. I couldn't imagine the client having a need for this amount. I phoned the account head office and asked if they could give me any information about the withdrawal. They couldn't give such information out unless I wrote in officially. I had no choice but to write in as they requested, and I got the Social Services Director to sign the letter.

When she came back from her "holiday" I invited her in to discuss the withdrawal from Mrs King's account.

50

She denied any wrongdoings again repeating that she had "won" the holiday. I told her that I felt it necessary to investigate the matter further, and that it would involve a hearing meeting to which she could bring her union representative should she wish to do so. Two weeks later when given the date of the hearing she threatened me with the union and said she would be bringing their highest representative.

The meeting was scheduled and eight people sat round the table to discuss the issue.

Our best piece of evidence was the response from the Scottish Bank. They clearly recognized that the signature on the withdrawal was not that of the account holder. They sent two copies of each. When this evidence was produced the union representative asked to be allowed to go out of the room with the helper. He returned with her resignation. There was nothing we could do to recoup the money, as we had no admittance of guilt. The good news was that the union had insurance for such events and they paid out just under the amount lost.

Later that year I heard that the helper had a new job in the ticket office of the local cinema! She must have had unfettered access to the till!

The Outing

The helpers decided that they would like to go on a group outing and asked me to think up some choices for them to select.

It was in the heyday of the Black and White Minstrels so that was one choice. The others were a London show like The Mousetrap, or an Ice Show. I sent off the list of suggestions to the four committee members and awaited their response.

As far as they were concerned none of the choices were suitable so I told them to find out what most helpers wanted and to let me know.

Two weeks later the answer arrived they wanted to go to London to some club in Soho and see "King Dick", the then famous male stripper.

What could I say, after all I had left the decision to them. So I arranged a coach, and forty seats in the club and off we went. I honestly didn't know what to expect. If I say the evening was the most riotous time I have ever spent I would not be lying. The warm up act just prior to

"King Dick" was preposterous. He was called "Mr Bubbles" He came on stage sporting a jacket that had fairy lights all over it. They blinked on and off, and I wondered where he kept the batteries. Then he stripped down to his pants and bubbles floated all around him. His mother certainly didn't use Persil to wash his underwear! Then as he twirled around he slipped in the bubble mixture and fell flat on his back. He must have hurt himself for the canned music stopped and he hobbled off his act unfinished.

I have to say that the star of the show was really good. He had us in stitches with his jokes and naughty innuendos.

We got home outside the office at about one o'clock in the morning. The helpers were still in very high spirits and a lot of ribald laughing was still going on.

Apparently there were two complaints to the police about the noise from residents as we left the coach, but luckily nobody found out who it was who caused the incident.

The Wig Wearer

One of my more glamorous home helps loved to wear enormous and colourful wigs. She had an ash blonde, a raven black, a silver grey and a bright red one. She had names for them all. The blonde one was Dolly, the brown one was Whitney, the black one was Drusilla, and the red one Shirley

I had some reservations about this when she first commenced work with us but she proved to be a really good helper.

However, some people realized that she wore wigs whilst others did not. She coped with most of our male clients. They all seemed to love the variations in her looks. One elderly lady who got used to her with black hair was suddenly faced with a blonde did not recognise that she was her usual helper and rang me in great distress because I had taken away her regular helper whom she liked, but did not like this new one at all. No matter how hard I tried she would not have the blonde back but readily accepted the black-haired one.

This helper also had a variety of clip on nails which she decorated with amazing patterns. I couldn't imagine doing housework and shopping with such long nails but she managed and the clients loved it. At one of her female clients request she even painted the elderly lady's toenails in a gold and black zigzag pattern for her. The client's son was furious when he saw them and rang up to complain. I had to inform him that his mother had specifically asked for this to be done. I tried to get him to see that his mother was really happy with her newly decorated toes and that he should appreciate that even older ladies liked to be pampered. If only he hadn't been the local bank manager!

Ding Dong Bell

On a visit to a client way out in the wilds, I noticed that her oil-fired Aga was leaking onto the wooden kitchen floor. Next to the leak stain was a five gallon drum of paraffin for all her other heaters.

I felt a bit concerned that the leak and the drum being so close to the heat source of the Aga was not a good idea. I looked round the bungalow to try and find somewhere else for the paraffin drum to be stored, but because the house was so cluttered with heavy old Victorian furniture there was little choice elsewhere. I had a talk with the helper who, had brought the situation to my notice, hence my visit. Her answer was that she thought we should leave the decision to her son who although he lived in London, often came down at the weekend to visit.

I phoned him when I got back to the office and he agreed that it was dangerous, and that he would see what he could do on Saturday when he came down.

'You see,' I said, 'I have the safety of my staff to consider as well as your mother's.'

That phrase would live to haunt me.

The son did visit on Saturday and he did move the paraffin drum. He put it right up at the top of the garden in a derelict wooden shed.

So the poor helper had to hack her way through the undergrowth to get paraffin for the heaters in rain and snow. It was not a pleasant task.

However, it was to get much worse. One day in the middle of winter after a particularly heavy snowfall, and after she had abandoned her car, and walked almost two miles through the drifts to get to Mrs. Martin, she went up to the shed to get some fuel, and on the way back to the house she trod on the old wooden cover of the well, hidden beneath the snow. It gave way and she fell down the well.

The poor woman wasn't too deeply down but could not reach the top with her arms to pull herself out. She thought it would be impossible to summon any help as she was far from the house anyway. But Lady Luck was definitely on her side that morning for the postman walked past the property and heard her calling for help. He managed to pull her out and help her into the house. She wasn't really hurt. She had a couple of bruises on her arms and a scraped shin. The well was only about six feet deep and dry of water.

Sometime later she and the son had a good laugh about the incident. He replaced the well cap with a metal one.

But the adventure had an unexpected and romantic ending, because the helper and the postman became an item, and after a year they were married. She laughed and said that she fell for him in a big way.

Water, Water, but not Anywhere

Oh here we go, I thought as I pulled up outside the old wooden cottage. Why do all these elderly ladies seem to live in these awful unmodernised properties?

I knocked at the door and waited. It was absolutely freezing, and the east wind was blowing snow flurries directly from the sea. By the time the lady had managed to totter to the door I must have looked like a yeti standing out in the snow.

Her lounge which was the only main room in the house was filled to the brim with heavy dark Victorian furniture. Each side of the tiled fireplace was an armchair both of which had certainly been well used over the years.

The lady herself was clad in brown from head to toe and layers and layers of cardigans made her look bigger than she really was. The fire was alight although it seemed to be struggling to throw out any warmth.

'You poor thing having to come all this way out in this weather,' she said. 'I'd make you a nice cup of tea but, of course, I can't because my water is frozen. It's been like that for days now.'

'May I look in your kitchen?'

'Of course you can, my dear.' She followed me out to the scullery. There was an old butler sink but I noticed immediately that there were no taps connected to it.

'Where is your water?'

'Oh it's outside, out on the wall. It comes from a tap but in the cold weather it always gets frozen up.'

'How do you manage then? Have you got a container to store some water in.?

'No dear. If I stored some I wouldn't be able to carry it would I?'

I went outside and looked at the mains tap, sure enough it was covered in icicles and obviously frozen solid.

After we talked about the kind of help she needed and I arranged for it to start the next day I ensured that the helper took a water container with her. Meanwhile I persuaded my ever-willing husband to go up and look at the pipes. He said he could run the water inside to the kitchen sink quite easily. Which he did. Mrs Owen was so thrilled she almost skipped round the kitchen.

'I've always had outside water,' she said. 'I never imagined I would get it inside. I will have to tell my son he will be pleased'.

'Your son?' I asked.

'Oh yes he comes here at least twice a year to see me; he really is so very kind.'

What could I say? Kind wasn't the adjective I would have applied to a son who left his mother with an outside tap.

'How does your toilet work in this weather? My husband asked as he gathered his tools up.

'Oh that's outside too. It's frozen at the moment but I use a chamber pot indoors. I empty it down the outside toilet but, of course, I cannot flush it away in this weather.'

We both looked at each other. No words were spoken but I knew instinctively that the frozen pipes were about to be lagged.

As we prepared to leave I happened to ask her what her son did for a living.

'Oh he's a plumber in London. I understand he's earning really good money.'

We both left in a hurry before either of us said something we might regret.

When I spoke to her son about the water, he admitted that his mother had a problem with the outside supply, but that he felt if he modernized it she wouldn't be so high up on the council's rehousing list.

There was no polite answer so I said nothing. Later my husband re-plumbed the toilet pipes which never froze again.

Some People Just Can't be Helped

Mr. Phillips had been some kind of important person in the Diplomatic Service. He lived in an untidy flat filled with stacks of newspapers and books, which it was difficult to walk past without dislodging something.

He was furious that his doctor had asked me to visit and told me in no uncertain terms that as a woman I was of no useful purpose whatsoever.

That went down well!

It took me about an hour to persuade him to accept one visit a week to help him to create some living space so that he could sit in his armchair and eat at the table.

'If you send me some dope of a woman I won't let her in.'

'I don't have any male helpers, but the lady I am thinking of sending here is a very experienced helper and I'm sure once you get used to her you will find the company useful.'

'I've never met a useful woman yet,' was all he had to say.

To say he was awful to the helper is an understatement. I spent the next six months constantly going to his flat to tell him off for his insulting behaviour and his downright rudeness.

I decided to put the home helps on a rota so that nobody would have to suffer his behaviour week in week out. He hated this, of course, and wrote to the prime minister to complain, blaming it all on me and my incompetence.

Interestingly, all his post was delivered without stamps, and by hand from the post office. The poor postman was constantly climbing up the stairs to our third floor office to hand deliver a missive from Mr. Phillips. His deliveries had to be signed for by the designated recipient only.

One of the helpers on the rota happened to mention that I was going on holiday to Greece the following week. I was very, very nervous about my first flight and my fears were made significantly worse when the postman delivered a card from Mr. Phillips. It said that he hoped that I was aware that planes often plummeted out of the sky for no apparent reason, and that he hoped mine would.

It didn't, and upon my return from holiday refreshed and ready for a showdown, I engaged my boss, to accompany me to his Mr. Phillips's flat.

After an hour-long angry yelling session about the uselessness of me and my team the director decided to withdraw his service on the grounds of his unreasonable behaviour and we waited for the fallout. This was the one and only time that service was withdrawn from a client, and I didn't feel good about it.

We received a letter from Buckingham Palace asking for details of the case. The director answered the letter and we heard no more.

I still felt somewhat responsible for the withdrawal, because I felt that if I could have established a rapport with him we could have sorted some proper help regime up to suit his needs, after all he was a very intelligent man and there must have been something in his life that we could have latched onto to make his anger less aggressive.

Petty Arguments

Why is it I wonder that the smaller the value of something the greater the argument about it.

Miss Quinn was the epitome of a Victorian spinster. She was very tall and slim, beautifully dressed at all times, and usually sported a lace-ruff like neckpiece on all her dresses. She stared down at everyone with a fixed look of disdain. Especially at me because I'm quite short.

Her bungalow was in one of the sought after areas of the island, detached and set in an immaculate garden. She was well off and had a gardener but no help in the house.

When I first visited she treated me like a servant. I knew with her attitude she would be difficult to help, but I selected a nice middle class helper whom I was sure would fit in well.

All she wanted was one visit for shopping and one for wielding the hoover. All went well for quite a time. On my second visit which was to see how she liked the service or not, she spent ages telling me she was the aunt of a very famous TV personality who was currently starring in a very popular comedy series. There were photos of him all round the walls and on the sideboard.

One afternoon when I just happened to be in the office, the phone rang and my clerk whispered that this TV star was on the phone.

As I put the phone to my ear he began a rampage of shouting about my helper stealing his auntie's property.

I asked him to explain in more detail what property we were talking about and that if he could calm down we would get to the point more rapidly.

He said he was not prepared to discuss it over the phone but that he was at his auntie's house now so it would be best if I could go up there immediately and we could have it out.

I have to be honest here and say that I didn't drive too quickly; I made him wait. When I entered the house he started.

'Your member of staff that you sent here to my frail and vulnerable auntie is dishonest, and had purloined something that belongs to her. She is rightly very upset.

'She has stolen my stamps,' Auntie piped up.

'Stamps?'

'Yes, you know the supermarket in the village gives us stamps for each pound spent and they are stuck into a book and spent at some other time like Christmas. The helper has stolen stamps that are rightly mine. She waved several filled stamp books in my face.

'Look, see this book. I spent nineteen pounds and I should have nineteen stamps but I've only got eighteen.'

'Are we discussing one stamp here?'

'One stamp or one hundred stamps what matters is the principle of the thing,' he interjected.

As the helper lived close by I said I would call round and discuss the stamp with her.

She was furious as I expected.

'I put one stamp in to fill up the old book, then, I left the eighteen on the table for Miss Quinn to put in herself, in the new book, because she likes doing it.

'I'm not happy to go there again if she thinks I'm a thief.'

I went back to the house and explained what the helper had said, and was told in no uncertain terms not to provide any further help.

I went over to the shop to enquire the value of the stamps.

'They are worth two pence each I suppose,' said the shop assistant. Customers can have one for every pound spent. If it's Miss Quinn you are enquiring for we have already had her nephew over here ranting and raving about the bloody things. Sometimes they are more trouble than they're worth.

I knew exactly what she meant. Incidentally, I never watched any of his programmes again.

A Bash Over the Head

Mr. Rogers used to be the only dental surgeon on the island. He was famous for his dapper appearance. He always wore a black suit and a bow tie, his shoes always shone and he was very gracious and polite to everyone.

He lived in a grand terraced three storey house, in a leafy avenue, opposite the church.

After his retirement he deteriorated rapidly. I supplied him with a helper who kept him on his toes for quite a while.

He began to forget to dress in the morning, or to change his clothes if he had bothered to dress. He became unkempt and dirty. His language descended into vile outbursts of swearing. He would swear at the churchgoers on Sundays, and yell at people in the street. It was really sad to see such a pillar of the community sink to such depths.

He rang me one morning ranting on about his helper having stolen a knife full of butter from his butter dish. I popped round as he wasn't far from the office, in the hope that I could calm him down. The helper was there when I arrived and she was calm and collected.

'I don't worry about his accusations,' she said, 'he doesn't really mean them.'

Mr. Rogers showed me his butter dish. There was a scrape of butter missing from the top of the block.

'Is nothing sacred,' he yelled, 'If a man can't rely on his fucking butter dish being safe what else is being stolen?'

'You had the butter on your breakfast toast and marmalade Mr. Rogers.' the helper said.

'Oh, yes I forgot my breakfast. Did you have it with me?' he asked me.

'No I had mine at my house.'

'Allow me to show you out, Madam,' he said in his old posh voice.

Picking up his Zimmer frame he followed me to the front door. I opened the door and as I stood on the threshold the most amazing thump hit the back of my head and I couldn't for the moment imagine what had happened.

Mr. Rogers had held his Zimmer frame up in the air behind me and brought it crashing down on my head. Luckily for me it was made of soft aluminium and Mr, Rogers was weak so it didn't do any damage but it did shock me that such a man could do a thing like that.

A Bribe Refused

It's not often in a job like mine that one is faced with a deliberate bribe, but one year as Christmas approached that's exactly what happened to me. I was visiting a very well-off lady on a routine visit. Her bungalow had carpets so thick that my ankles disappeared in the pile. Shining silver objects were festooned on all possible surfaces. She had a helper with whom she was very pleased.

I have to be honest and say I always found it more difficult to assess the help needed for well off clients than the poorer ones. It was so much more obvious what was required for those whose life had deteriorated. But I was once told by a very rich lady that her inability to clean her silver was as depressing as not being able to do housework.

Miss Sampson asked me if it was possible for her to go into one of our care homes for Christmas as she was to be alone again and hated the long "period of silence", as she put it. As there was only three weeks to go before the festive season it was going to be impossible for me to find a vacancy. Lonely people usually booked a place months ahead of time. I explained this to Miss Sampson, but promised that should a cancellation come up I would put her name forward. I picked up my bag to leave, and as I got into my car my bag bumped noisily onto the side of the door. I couldn't imagine what had made the noise. As I strapped my safety belt on I looked I into my bag. Horror of horrors it contained a silver candelabra. I couldn't get out of my car quickly enough I hammered on Miss Sampson's door.

'You cannot do things like this Miss Sampson. I really am very cross with you.'

She just smiled and said, 'I thought it might help.'

'Well it won't,' I snapped.

I plunged the offending candelabra back into her hands and drove away. Imagine what would have been said if I had driven off with the blasted thing.

As it happened there was a cancellation at the last minute and Miss Sampson took the place eagerly. When I next visited her to collect the payment for her stay she said it wasn't as enjoyable as she expected. There was too much noise at night and she couldn't sleep, and the permanent residents seemed to object to the visiting ones and wouldn't speak to them. She then admitted that the problem of mixing in was probably hers as she had "lost the art" of mixing and conversing with strangers.

So, I guess next year I won't be offered any silver.

I'm Going To Do It

The referral for Mrs. Thomas said and I quote. "Lady is a "bit of a pot sui", needs some domestic help." Having no idea what a bit of a pot sui meant I didn't hurry out. I left it till the next day. I thought it was some kind of Chinese takeaway, *but* it meant "potential suicide". I do wish doctors wouldn't use their own shorthand for issues.

Mrs. Thomas appeared to be reasonably happy to see me and we had an animated conversation about the kind of help we could offer and what her immediate needs were. Then she reached the subject of her son: her only son whom she had obviously adored.

'He married a girl from Australia. She was a student at the same university as him. They didn't want to live here on the island, I can understand that, but then he phoned to say they were going to Australia. I said "that will be a nice holiday for you, Malcolm", and he said, "no, Mum we are going for good."

At this point she burst into tears and buried her head in her hands.

'I'm sorry, Mrs. Thomas when was this? Just recently?'

'It must be five years ago now,' she replied looking across at a calendar on the wall.

'Has he been home since?' I asked knowing what the answer might be.

'No, he says they can't afford the trip. I've offered to pay their fare, but they just don't have the time. I can't see much reason for me to carry on like this. My husband died six years ago and now my son has gone there's nothing to keep me on this earth is there?'

'Oh, I don't know Mrs. Thomas, look round at your lovely home and all your personal belongings. You are certainly very lucky compared to some of the ladies I meet.' I realised that it must have sounded a bit patronising and wouldn't be of much help.

'Maybe when you get used to a helper coming in you will have someone to talk to and engage with. Some of my staff lead very interesting lives you know.'

She got a really nice helper and all went well for quite a while, but as Christmas approached she became monosyllabic and very depressed.

Her helper phoned to say she was worried with Christmas fast approaching, it meant that Mrs. Thomas would have gone without help for almost eight days.

The helper asked if she might pop in on a purely voluntary basis over the Christmas time, and I agreed.

On Christmas afternoon the helper found Mrs. Thomas dead in the armchair. She left a note to apologise for her suicide and hoped her helper would find replacement work. Not a mention of her son. She left her property and bank balance to a local charity for homeless dogs and cats.

Her son spent ages contesting the will but lost out in the end. He didn't even have the decency to come over for her funeral. The home help and I were the only ones there.

A Lovely Gift

Now I know that this story has appeared in the local newspaper and then repeated by others but I can assure you its origin was in our group.

One of my helpers worked for ages with a really dirty and disheveled elderly man. Mr. Underwood was a charmer of the highest order. He was always ready with a quip or a joke. He read the papers every morning in the library, much to the disgust of the staff and other readers, and would hold debates with his helper on all sorts of world issues.

Just before she stopped for Christmas he presented her with a little parcel wrapped in clean tissue paper and tied with a pink ribbon.

'Just a little something to show my appreciation,' he said.

'Wow. Thank you, Mr. Underwood. I shall take it home and open it on Christmas morning.'

Off she went clutching her little gift. On Christmas morning she duly opened the parcel to find a see-through plastic container filled to the brim with shiny whole brazil nuts. She had no intention of sharing her gift with her three kids or her other half, so over the three days of the Christmas break she secretly devoured all the nuts, thoroughly enjoying them. Upon returning to work she thanked Mr. Underwood for his lovely gift.

'I really enjoyed them. Where did you get them?'

'Oh I won them in a raffle down the pub,' he said. 'They were covered in milk chocolate when I got them, but I sucked all that chocolate off, and as I couldn't eat the nuts with my teeth I thought of you.'

It was at that moment that the helper wished she had shared her gift with everyone else in the family.

Hard to Find and Even Harder to Get to

As I said before I hate debt collecting, but apparently Mr. Vincent owed almost three hundred pounds to social services and even more to the local council. I hasten to add these debts were accrued prior to my time in post. I never let anyone build up an unpayable debt. So I set off with his address on my passenger seat.

I passed a farm worker trimming a huge long hedge, and turned right as the signpost directed just a bit further down the lane.

Several minutes later I passed the same worker and the same hedge. Back down to the crossroads and turned right again. Round the lane I went and, yes, I came back to the hedge and the farm worker.

This time I stopped and asked him the way to the village.

'Turn left at the crossroads.' he said.

'But the signpost says the village is to the right.'

He thought for a moment and then he smiled and said, 'Oh, yes, I hit the signpost with my tractor last week and it swiveled round. I just forgot to put it back.'

Down to the crossroads I went, for the third time, turned right instead of left, and found the village I required.

But I just couldn't find the address. So I knocked at the door of a huge farmhouse.

The posh lady who answered the door told me that the address I was seeking was where their orchard used to be.

I thanked her and set off again before realizing that there was no indication of where their orchard used to be.

However, after some time I found a sign written on an old bit of plywood that pointed across a ploughed field, to the name of the house I needed.

I always have a pair of wellies in the boot so I donned them and struggled across the muddy field to the house. There was no access to the house, even the land round it was ploughed right up to the front door and all around the walls. The ruts were deep and water filled. By the time I reached the door I looked like Worzel Gummage on a good day.

I knocked on the door and it was opened by a frail white-haired man. I explained why I was there and he invited me inside. The house was huge and full of beautiful furniture. Mr. Vincent cried as he explained to me the stresses he was under. The house had been in his family for generations, but he didn't own the access, it was rented from the farmer who ploughed the land.

'He wants me out so he can demolish the house and keep the land ploughed. Hence, the ploughing right up to my door.'

'I can't get my car out of the barn to go into town,' he said. 'The doctor won't visit, nobody will deliver anything, I have to get across the field even to get the milk.'

I couldn't bring myself to ask about his debts. I was more interested in seeing if there was any way to help him with his access problems.

'If only I had some way to raise some cash I could pay off all my debts and rent arrears and the bloody farmer wouldn't have a leg to stand on in getting me out.'

He made me a cup of tea and we sat chatting for a while. It wasn't until I mentioned my husband's love of classic cars that he brightened up.

'I've got three lovely old girls in the barn. Would you like to see them?

'Yes, please.'

We both donned wellies and out we went to the barn. Inside were three of the most beautiful but neglected classic cars I had seen in a long time. There was a Jaguar, a Daimler and an original Second World War American jeep with all its fittings. They were covered in about an inch of dust but they were amazing.

'Well, Mr. Vincent you don't need to worry about your debts; just one of these cars sold at auction would make you enough money to do what you want.'

'Do you really think so?'

'Look, I will pop a car magazine to you in the post, it has lists of auction houses who would give their right arm to have one of these in their sale.'

I did just that and three months later he sent a thank you card to the office and a cheque for his debts. I smiled and wondered which of his beloved classics had done the trick.

The next time I went past the house I was relieved to see a newly constructed tarmac driveway, and Mr. Vincent's Daimler outside the front door.

Obviously the Jaguar and the jeep had provided him with some much needed cash.

A Lethal Bath

Occasionally clients could have been better off if I hadn't visited.

This particular couple were referred for some domestic help as the wife was very tottery on her feet and kept falling over.

The house was a normal terrace in a normal road, so I wasn't expecting any major problems. The main room was warm, clean and tidy, although rather cluttered. It led out into the old fashioned scullery where I could see one of those long tin baths that our grandparents used to have. I glanced at it and saw Mr. Williams filling it with water directly from the sink's one tap. I didn't think about it being cold water.

As I sat and discussed what Mrs. Williams would like in the way of help, she called out to her husband, 'Don't forget to put the immersion in dear, then you can come in here and meet this nice lady while the water heats up.'

He came into the room and we all sat and talked about life in general. Then Mr. Williams got up to go and have his bath. As I looked round my heart leapt into my mouth. There hanging from a ceiling light cable was an immersion heater dangling into the bath water!

'Mr. Williams is not going to get into that bath with the immersion heater like that is he?'

'He'll be all right dear,' she replied.

I couldn't leave without demanding that they took the immersion out of the water before he got in.

When I got back to the office I phoned the electricity board to ask for advice on how to deal with what I had seen. I do wish I hadn't phoned for they rushed round there with a huge lorry and cut off the couple's supply. I had to organize a generator and some gas cooking appliances while the whole of their house was rewired for safety.

I suppose it was all for the better in the long run.

A Scruffy Helper

One of my helpers was very scruffy. She always looked as though her uniform overall had been in a chip fat fight. I used to cross the road or hide in a shop doorway if I saw her coming along the street. Yet she was a godsend to me with many of the tatty elderly male clients we had who all seemed to live in the ghetto-like part of the town where the council dumped all the "undesirables".

Her time sheet was always filled in with a particular style of writing which quite honestly didn't seem to match with her. It was very modern in and very carefully scripted.

She came into the office one day to ask about some extra help for one of her clients when my clerk asked her to sign her last week's timesheet.

She went very red and scribbled an illegible scrawl at the base of her sheet. This didn't match with all her usual signatures. I followed her down the stairs as she left and enquired about the signature. She admitted then that she could neither read nor write and that her daughter had been filling in her time sheet.

'I suppose that means you will sack me now.' She said.

'Of course not,' I said, 'why would I want to sack you? We will just make a note on your file and continue to accept you daughter's writing.

'Would you like me to teach you to read?' I enquired, after all I was a schoolteacher before I came here.'

'No thanks, I've managed up till now so I will go on as I am thanks. My daughter is helping me read a bit, and it doesn't affect my ability to do my job. Does it?'

'No, it certainly doesn't,' I replied.

Dead and Forgotten

One of our clients who only had one visit a week for shopping was not answering her door. The helper came round and together we went to the house. It was a terraced house in the midst of a long row.

As we knocked at the door the neighbour came out and said that the television had been blaring for three days and nights and was a "bloody nuisance". I tried to peer through the netting at the windows but was unable to see anything. I told the helper to go on to her next client and went round to the police station for someone to come with me and break in. Social services do not have authority to break into people's houses.

A policeman came and together we broke a small window. He felt for the opening of the bigger window and we climbed in. Mrs. Xavier was dead in an armchair in front of the very hot television. We switched it off. I had brought her information card with me so we looked for a relative's contact number. There was an address but no telephone number. The policeman said he would go round to what appeared to be the daughter's house and see if anyone was in. It was only two streets away. He came back with a very harassed looking woman. I assumed she was distressed to hear about her mother's demise but apparently not.

'What the bloody hell did she want to go and die today for, she knows how busy I am. Wednesday is my only day off.'

'I don't suppose she wanted to die today,' I said, 'has she been unwell?'

'I don't know, she never said anything.'

'When was the last time you saw her?' asked the policeman.

'Oh, I don't know, a couple of weeks ago I suppose. Why?'

'I'm trying to establish when she was last seen alive. That's all.'

Then she noticed the window.

'Who broke the bloody window? You had better pay to have it mended because I'm not going to.'

I left the policeman with the lovely daughter and went back to the office to arrange for the window to be boarded over.

Three weeks later the funeral parlour boss phoned to ask me what I was proposing to do with Mrs. Xavier's body.

'What do you mean what am I going to do with it?

'Well we haven't had communication with anyone about the arrangements.'

'She has a daughter and this is her address, I suggest you contact her and insist that she makes all necessary arrangements. But don't call in the day unless it's a Wednesday as she is very busy.'

I bet she was a pleased as punch when he called round.

Sherry in abundance, but no Food

There's a certain group of people, mainly ladies, who have led a very middle class life, and now live in the large family houses that their families used to occupy. One such lady was Mrs. Zenova she presented herself as what I call the "genteel" poor. She was painfully thin, and fragile. She lived in a three-storey seafront house. She was a tiny little lady who looked so out of place in the large bay windowed rooms that she showed me round. As the clock on the mantelpiece chimed eleven she went straight to the glass cabinet, selected two crystal glasses and without even asking me, poured out two huge sherries.

I'm not a sherry lover, in fact it makes me shudder, but I held my glass politely, as we discussed her life. She had been the only daughter of a professional couple. Her two brothers had emigrated to Australia and she only got a Christmas card each year from them. She had nursed her mother for years after her father died, and consequently never got the chance to marry. She had lived alone in this huge house for over fifty years. When she showed me into the kitchen I noted that there was no fridge, and that the three-shelved larder had one jar of marmite in solitary glory sitting on the middle shelf.

'What do you like to eat?' I asked.

'Eat?' she said as if I'd asked her how many times she had sex per week.

'I eat whatever is in the house.'

'But Miss Zenovia, there isn't anything in the house.'

'Is there not?' she said sipping her sherry. 'I must have forgotten to get something in.'

'Would you like some help with shopping say once a week?'

'Oh no, I don't think so. I mean what would I get her to fetch. I've got everything I want.'

You can't force people to have help even if you know that they need it, so I left my card and she promised to call if she needed anyone in the future.

My sherry?

It was poured very gently into the huge potted fern, while she wasn't looking. I expect it survived.

Two Bonus Tales I just had to Include

I was invited to go and give a talk about the Home Help Service to a church group of older parishioners.

I found the church hall and had just introduced myself to the seated group when an elderly man in the front row pitched out of his chair and fell at my feet.

I could see from his colour that this was a medical emergency, so I got one of the helpers in the kitchen area to run across the road and call for an ambulance.

I began to try and resuscitate the man whilst we waited for the ambulance. It was very prompt, but in those days the crews were not paramedics like they are today. They had basic first aid training and some medical equipment.

As the two men inserted an oxygen pipe and set up the pump, I continued to press his chest at their command. Whilst in the middle of this and while we were all concentrating on our efforts, one of the ladies knelt down and poked her head between us and said.

'We usually have a cup of tea at three and it's three now.'

'You best go and make it then,' I said rather sharply.

'Oh, I don't make it there are two ladies who do that.'

'Well go and get them to make it then.' And off she went.

The two ambulance men looked at me but there was no need for any words.

I heard later that the man did not survive our attempts to save him, but we did try very hard.

After Eight Mints

My husband and I went to a Christmas Party at one of the residential homes. The helpers had been asked to bring any one of their clients that they knew would be able to manage such an outing.

The large room was decked out with brightly coloured baubles and strings of resident's homemade decorations.

There was a piano at which sat a very elderly lady sporting a deaf aid in each ear. I couldn't help wondering what she could hear.

Then a gentleman stood up to play the trombone. I think they were supposed to be playing the same piece of music but the pianist galloped along with her interpretation and the trombonist kept stopping as he ran out of breath. When he started again he went on from where he had stopped, but by then the pianist was pages ahead of him. The resulting noise was awful, but we clapped with enthusiasm when the end was at last reached.

I thought I would help the ladies in the kitchen to deliver the snacks so I carried a huge plate filled with little sausage rolls which I placed on a table next to some residents. I turned to look at something else and when I turned back, no more than a couple of seconds later, the plate was completely empty. I couldn't imagine where the sausage rolls had gone. One of the care staff came running up and said.

'Oh, no! You didn't put the sausage rolls near Gerald did you?'

'I don't know, who is Gerald?

'That's Gerald there, next to the table. You see Gerald has an eating disorder.'

'Yes, it's an eating disorder that means he eats anything he sees. He has to be kept right away from food unless it is handed to him by one of us. He isn't a resident of the home but he comes in each day so that we can control his diet.

At the end of the evening there was a raffle and I won a box of After Eight Mints. As the party wound up I was asked if we would give Gerald and his carer a lift home as we would be passing their house.

As I drove away with Gerald and his carer in the back my husband, who had missed the sausage roll event, opened the chocolates, gave me one, took one himself and passed the box back to the carer.

Well, we had never heard such a noise in all our lives. Gerald snatched the box from his carer and devoured the mints, paper and all. But that wasn't the end. He then devoured the box!

Every time I see a box of After Eight Mints now even after all these years I can't help but think of Gerald.

A Word From the Author

A word or two about me. I assume you have gathered by now that I was in charge of providing services to elderly people on the Isle of Sheppey, in Kent.

I am a qualified teacher but I left when I saw the job of Home Services Manager advertised. So I moved from five-plus year olds to seventy-five-plus year olds.

What I enjoyed most was the freedom from the classroom. If I needed to buy a loaf of bread I could buy one when I passed a bakers shop at any time of the day.

OK I didn't have the whole of August off, or half terms etc, but I really didn't mind. One thing that must be pointed out is that these were the days before mobile phones, and advanced telecommunications. Most of my clients did not have a telephone. Those town dwellers could get one, at a price, but out in the wilds there was no way any of them apart from the very rich could afford to have the lines put in. When and if I had to call an ambulance or a doctor it was a case of finding the nearest telephone box, or a householder with a phone who was willing to let me make a call.

My team of home helps were the salt of the earth. They would put up with all sorts of verbal and physical abuse to help their clients. They coped with filthy houses, flea infestations, houses full of cats, or dogs, rooms full of excrement, naked men and women, flooded homes, burst hot water cylinders, frozen pipes. You name it they had seen it all. Because of the lack of communications they mostly coped with difficult situations themselves and then came into the office to let me know, or phoned from their own home.

They were, and probably still are, an underrated medal-deserving group, and I miss them all.

The joy of the job, and it was a real joy, was taken away when some central government bright spark decided to split the assessment of need from the provision of the service. I think the supposition was that thousands of pounds would be saved. This meant that I would have to visit to assess an individual's need, but ask someone else to provide the response. In fact, I would no longer be sure that the service had been provided.

The supplier, or commissioner, as they were called would not meet the clients, so matching was hit and miss. Imagine what it would be like to have a helper come into your home and the two of you just didn't like each other for some reason.

The helpers left in droves and most of them went to work in local factories or shops.

We bid each other an emotional and tearful farewell, and I went to head office to pastures new.